Learning to Be a Good Friend

A Guidebook for Kids

Written by
Christine A. Adams

Illustrated by
R. W. Alley

ONE
CARING
PLACE

Abbey Press
St. Meinrad, IN 47577

D1401253

To my grandkids, who are wonderful friends!

Edward Harrison Hanley
Benjamin Michael Firsick
James Eliot Firsick
Grace Lenore Christine Hanley
Diana Mary Butch
Katie Butch

Text © 2004 Christine A. Adams
Illustrations © 2004 St. Meinrad Archabbey
Author photo by Marilee Frazier, Santa Monica, California
Published by One Caring Place
Abbey Press
St. Meinrad, Indiana 47577

Library of Congress Catalog Number
2004111076

ISBN 0-87029-388-5

Printed in the United States of America

A Message to Parents, Teachers, and Other Caring Adults

All kids need friends. To have friends, a child needs to learn to *be* a good friend. Yet children aren't born with finely tuned social skills. They need to learn how to make friends, choose friends wisely, and keep good friends.

The single most important factor in the development of friendship skills is the way children are treated at home and school. Attitudes of acceptance versus criticism in these environments get played out in the child's social world. For example, constantly demanding things of a child instead of negotiating decisions can teach that child to be bossy and demanding with peers.

Second, adults can teach children to be kind to themselves when they make mistakes. In turn, these children will learn to be compassionate with other kids when they make mistakes. Through kindness and understanding, adults can show the child what it means to be a caring, supportive friend.

Third, adults can help children develop empathy for others. They can ask important questions at key times, like "How do you think Ryan felt when you said he was stupid?" By talking about the feelings and thoughts behind actions, kids can begin to recognize and take on the other person's viewpoint. A good follow-up question might be: "What can you do next time you feel that angry? What choices do you have?"

By letting kids know they have social options, grownups help them to avoid behaviors that deter friendship and lead to peer rejection. Many kids resort to inappropriate behaviors, like fighting or teasing, because they haven't mastered adaptive social skills. Kids depend on caring adults to help them master appropriate tactics for all kinds of social situations.

All kids need to be taught how to cultivate and nurture friendship. Through modeling positive behavior and talking with kids about the issues covered in this book, you can be what a child needs most—a true friend.

—*Christine A. Adams*

What Is Friendship?

"Friendship" means having friends. Everyone needs friendship in his or her life.

A friend is someone you have fun with. You need a friend to hide so that you can find him. You need a friend to hit the ball so you can catch it. Your friends often like the same things as you—maybe tennis or dinosaurs or Cub Scouts.

You can play with friends just about anywhere—in your house, in your neighborhood, at school recess, or on a sports team.

Having a friend makes you feel happy inside. It's nice to care about someone and know that he cares about you, too!

Choosing a Friend

Katie and Grace go to dance class together on Wednesdays. They both like to play house and dress their dolls in different clothes. Choose a friend who likes what you like.

Stay away from kids who do bad things— like making fun of other kids, being mean to animals, or telling lies. They can really get you into trouble. Just being around a mean kid—even if you're not doing anything bad— can get you in trouble sometimes.

How to Make Friends

Be friendly—say hi and smile. Tell a kid who seems nice that his social studies project is cool. See if he wants to play with you and what he'd like to play.

If you see kids playing a game, and a kid makes a good move, say, "Nice shot." Wait until the game slows down and then ask to play.

Always have a "fun attitude." Grab a ball and say, "Who wants to play?" If no one does, just go on to something else. Soon others might join you.

If you're shy, these things can be hard to do. Ask God to give you a "boost" of bravery. Making friends is worth it!

Playing on a Team

Ask your mom or dad if you can play on a sports team. Being a part of a team is a great way to find friends.

Be a "good sport" by doing your best for the team, and letting other kids play their own positions. If a kid misses a pitch, a goal, or a basket, don't make fun. Just say, "Nice try."

Ask your parents if one of your new friends can come over to your house sometime to play with you.

How to Be a Friend

To have friends, you need to BE a friend. This means sharing, taking turns, and being fair. Treat your friends the way you want to be treated.

If you want to jump on the trampoline but your friend wants to play whiffleball, maybe you could play ball for fifteen minutes and then do the trampoline.

Do nice things for your friend. If she falls on the trampoline, say, "Are you all right?" and help her up. If she misses some words on the spelling test, tell her she'll do better next time.

How to Keep Friends

If you tell your friend you'll save a place for him at lunch, be sure to do it. Keeping promises is an important part of friendship.

If someone says something mean about your friend, stick up for him. If you hurt your friend in some way, say you're sorry and try to make it up to him.

If you and your friend don't agree about something, try to talk about it without getting mad. Really listen to your friend, so you can feel what he is feeling. See if the two of you can come up with a plan that works for both of you.

Things Friends Don't Do

Friends don't punch, kick, bite, or scratch each other. If you are wrestling or horsing around, be careful not to hurt your friend.

When you want a turn on the swing set, don't be mean and say, "If you don't let me swing, I won't be your friend."

Don't make fun of your friends—or anyone. Never use mean names or say bad things about someone behind her back. If you hurt someone's feelings, it's as bad as if you hit her. It hurts inside.

Be True to Yourself

Be yourself. You don't need to make up stories so other kids will like you. You don't need to look or act just like they do, so you can fit in with their group.

Just be honest and be true to yourself. If they don't like you the way you are, find some new friends who like you for who you really are.

If you have a group of friends you hang out with most of the time, don't be mean to other kids. It's okay to invite them to play with you, too. There's enough friendship in the world for everybody!

Do the Right Thing

When Peter ran over to his friends on the playground, he saw they were writing on the wall with markers. He knew this was wrong, but he did it anyway because his friends were doing it.

The janitor, who caught the boys, was mad. He said, "Who did this?" Only Peter and another kid admitted it. The others lied so they wouldn't get in trouble. Peter and his friend had to clean all the writing off the wall.

Never do something you know is wrong—even if all your friends are doing it.

Outsmarting a Bully

A bully is someone who is mean to other kids. If a bully is teasing you, pretend it doesn't bother you. Say, "I heard that one in kindergarten" or "Whatever." When you don't get upset, it takes the fun out of it, and the bully will stop.

If you are worried about being picked on, join up with another kid. Then go ask someone else to play with you. Bullies don't usually bother groups of kids.

Don't let a bully take your lunch money or things. Play near other kids or near the adult on the playground. Always tell your parents if a bully is picking on you. When kids and grownups stand up to bullies, they quit.

Having a Best Friend

A best friend is someone you like better than anyone else. You sit together at lunch and hang out at recess. You play and sleep over at each other's houses.

Some kids have more than one best friend. They might have a best friend at school, a best friend at gymnastics, and a best friend in the neighborhood. It's okay to have one, several, or even no best friends.

Even if you do have a #1 best friend, it's good to play with other kids too. The more people you get to know, the more friends you will have!

Changing Friends

Maybe your good friend joins the swim team and doesn't have as much time now. She might even eat lunch with a new friend from the team, which hurts your feelings.

If that happens, it's okay. Invite other kids you know to sit with you and see how it goes. You can choose to have a lot of friends or just a few—it's up to you.

Sometimes a really good friend might move away. That will make you very sad. Get your friend's new address and write a letter. You can also e-mail or talk on the phone. Ask your mom or dad if you and your friend can visit each other sometime.

Forever Friends

Jenny and Jessy are sisters who are best friends. They spend afternoons dressing up and pretending to be princesses. They both have other friends, but at home they are best friends.

Brothers and sisters, moms and dads, grandparents, aunts, uncles, and cousins can be lots of fun and great friends. They will always love you and be there for you. Be sure to tell them how you feel about them.

Never forget that you also have a Forever Friend in God. God knows you better than anyone knows you, and loves you more than anyone loves you. Call on God when you are lonely or scared or need help. God cares about you and always has time to listen.

Sharing Friendship

As you practice the tips in this book, you will become a better friend. You will learn how to really care about others' feelings. You will be able to share glad and sad times with them.

You will find that it's fun to have friends of all different ages—and friends who may look, talk, and be very different from you. You will have friends that you keep for many years, and also new friends that you make day by day.

Always be on the lookout for someone who seems to need a friend. Invite him or her to hang out with you—and you both will have a new friend!

Christine A. Adams, M.A., has spent thirty-two years teaching and counseling teens. She is the author of two adult Elf-help books, *One-Day-at-a-time Therapy* and *Gratitude Therapy*. With her husband, Robert J. Butch, LCSW, she coauthored the Elf-help for Kids book, *Happy To Be Me: A Kid's Book About Self-esteem*. *Learning to Be a Good Friend*  was written in collaboration with Harrison Edward Hanley, her grandson, pictured here with the author.

R. W. Alley is the illustrator for the popular Abbey Press adult series of Elf-help books, as well as an illustrator and writer of children's books. He lives in Barrington, Rhode Island, with his wife, daughter, and son.